Counting Colors

Counting Colors

a journey through infertility

Poems by

Cheryl Boyer

Kelsay Books

Cover image: Eunice Warfel
Author photograph: Piper Warlick Photography

ISBN: 978-1-947465-56-5

Kelsay Books
Aldrich Press
www.kelsaybooks.com

in memory of Ted
(Theodore Donald Ziemer)
August 28, 1972–February 25, 1992
who believed in me before I knew how
and shared his vision
of fire-born gold all those years ago

and for Jim
who believes in me always

Acknowledgments

With thanks to editors of the following publications in which these poems (or different versions of them) are upcoming or first appeared:

The Main Street Rag: "Mother-in-law," and "Miscarriage"
A Quiet Courage: "Ember," and "Devoted"
Poetry in Plain Sight: "Paul"
Kakalak: "Clear," "40 mph," "Eat," and "Elizabeth"

With Gratitude~

First and foremost, Almighty God, for the ultimate blessing of children and even such things as humble and powerful as words.

Maureen Ryan Griffin, my mentor, friend, and midwife of my writing dreams. Many of my words would not exist without you.

My Under Construction buddies, you have encouraged me even when you didn't know I felt like giving up. Thank you for your laughter, your tears, and for being a steadfast part of my writing life.

Don and Euni Warfel, my parents. Thank you for your constant love, for walking this journey with us, and loving our kids almost as much as we do.

Josiah and Izzi, without you this collection of poems would not hold such utter joy. You are precious beyond words. I'd choose you again and again.

Jim, you nudged me, ever so gently, to take that first class in the midst of my grief and vulnerability. Your support and encouragement are never-ending. Thank you for believing in me and embracing all that comes with this writing life.

Contents

About the Author

Rehearsal

I spent my childhood
days playing house
imagining myself
a mother then begged
to babysit, not satisfied
with dolls and make believe.

At age nine, I cradled
the baby of my mother's
friend, barely moved
for sixty minutes as I relished
his weight in my arms.

Two years later, I played
my Saturdays away
caring for my neighbors'
children ages five and three
and one, claimed my twenty
dollars, turned around and sent
the money to a little girl
I sponsored in the Philippines,
a girl I always dreamed
I would one day meet.

At fourteen, I hovered
in the entryway to evening
vespers, offered my services
to strangers, acquaintances,
entertained children
while parents worshipped.

I spent my rosy youth
in practice for the family
I dreamed of,
went off to college,
met the boy I would marry,
the man I hoped would father
the children
I would never bear.

First Loss

We can't afford a baby, are still babes
ourselves, yet I hope
for two pink lines, not one.

But I am not pregnant.

When my husband gets home from work,
I am overcome by tears
before words escape my lips.

I tell him I'm not pregnant.

We console each other, list the reasons
we are thankful I am not
pretend to each other, and I'm afraid

I will never be pregnant.

Endometriosis

noun en·do·me·tri·osis \ en-dō-ˌmē-trē-ˈō-səs\

the presence and growth of functioning
endometrial tissue in places
other than the uterus that often results in severe
pain and infertility
                              —Merriam-Webster

a diagnosis
          I received at nineteen
                    before I married,
          weighted with pain
                    and risk of infertility,

a word
          looming over my
                    dream of motherhood,
          wrinkling in my memory
                    where its purpled scars remain

History

– 1992
At nineteen, one blight
on my right ovary
caused debilitating pain
and once removed
I soon convinced myself

I could forget

– 1997
Months blended
into years
until one January night
the excised pain returned,
I no longer had reprieve

too great to hope for

– 2000
Long-delayed,
this surgery revealed
no longer one black spot,
now cysts and lesions blocked
more than both my ovaries

yet I still could not give up

– 2003
One more surgery, proof of
organs fused together,
ovaries scarred far
beyond their years,
too damaged to produce

the life we wanted

Mother-In-Law

Are you pregnant?
she asks

across the land line
the only thing

she ever asks
before requesting her son

Her voice
untethers me

Miscarriage

Don't say
you understand
then ask us all
to go around the table
and say
what we are thankful for

I'll laugh out loud
(a bitter laugh
I know you can't understand)
when you tell me
at least our family
is sensitive

I'll tell you I am glad
you believe we're such a group
as I endure the growing belly
of my brother's wife
their baby due
in two short months

This Christmas
I'll watch the children
open gifts, play
crawl into their grandfather's lap
my child
the only one absent

Three Weeks Old

Our eyes meet,
or so I think,
but maybe he stares
right past me, unfocused,
as I intently gaze into his baby
not-quite blues.

I stare for an eternity,
refuse to remove
my eyes from his,

wonder if I'll ever see
my own eyes
reflected
the way I see my brother's
in his newborn son's.

As I Watch a Mother with Her Child

I am not *your* mother
brushing back your golden hair
so consumed by you
I find it hard to release
my too-tight grip
on your hand
your heart
your self
as you grow into
your own person
move beyond the circle
of my arms

But there is a child
somewhere
whose mother I could be
if I can release
my too-tight grip
on this singular dream
consume myself
with forming family
in a different way
enfold another's child
in the circle
of my arms

These Hands Have

flipped page after page of books I've read
   to someone else's child
scrubbed countless bottles, pushed packed strollers

chased away fire ants and fears
   of little ones who aren't my own
bandaged scraped knees, cradled stubby fingers

wrapped gift after gift with yards of pale paper, ribbon
   for other women's baby showers
cooked frequent meals, washed endless dishes

brushed away my tears, grasped
   my husband's hand
held the weight of empty years

Ember

Each and every cycle
month
after month
year
after year
I tried to quell my
longing
but my head could not guard
my heart
from its small spark
of anticipation
expectation
that fanned at the edges
of my vision
a pilot light refusing
to be snuffed
no matter how often
the flames
of hope were
doused

Remains

after Jane Hirshfield's *Orange Oil in Darkness*

This heartache
is an extra gift

not unbearable as it may seem.
There is beauty

in recognizing sorrow
for what it is –

the other half
revealing possibility.

Iron grief in time
dissolves.

Counting Colors

My dream of giving life
trickled away
month by month
year by year

counting off days
like colors on a calendar –
first turquoise, cerulean,
sky blue, so full of hope,

a sunny yellow
brightening with caution,
tangerine, magenta,
blood red,

and after that, envy
green for every
pregnant belly I detected
on my radar

each child's cry
in the checkout line
Mother's Day ads
depicting happy families

colors that refused to fade
across the years
but finally changed
their hue.

Calculation

Ten years, almost,
one hundred twenty cycles,
give or take,
I tracked my basal body temperature,
charted the perfect time
to make a baby,

studied my hubby's travel schedule,
figured how and if and when
I'd tag along to take advantage
of my ovulation window,

tallied days until I would deliver
if and when I might conceive,

imagined my belly round and full,
the flutter of a baby's movement
rather than an arc of pain,

envied those who shared
exciting news with family,
parked in the expectant mother's spot,
shopped for maternity clothes,
and flaunted the circumference
of growing baby bumps.

I fingered so-soft baby clothes
in every store
and eyed mothers shopping
with their children

when all the while I envisioned
our child's blue eyes, fair skin, red hair,
my exhaustion after labor,
learning to breast feed.

I recovered from surgeries
meant to excise endometrial tissue
and its pain while still preserving
a thread of fertility,

curled up on the couch, in bed,
a hundred crumpled tissues on the floor
after another test read negative,
joked we should buy stock
in tissue and at-home pregnancy tests.

At tether's end, we decided to take a break,
a choice both frightening and wise,
while I tried to ignore my cycle,
near impossible after counted years.

We rediscovered one another,
a connection almost lost,
discussed, finally,
how and when, with whom,
to start the adoption process,
a different, daunting, draining task,

chose an agency,
completed reams of paperwork,
grappled with finances,
revealed ourselves to new strangers
in unfamiliar ways,

anticipated the arrival of our baby,
certain of this hope in a way
we'd never been before.

Incubation

I dig deep
in hard, cold ground
bury my grief
in darkness

but in winter's earth
waits a seed
watered by my tears

pushing upward
scudding, scraping
through solid

heavy ground
set to emerge
when least expected
breaking

into the unknown

Falling

after Maureen Ryan Griffin's *Symphony in E Minor:*
On Wanting the Leaves Off All the Trees

I am fragile
can't stand this sadness
that keeps beginning

that echoes
unresolved,
half over.

Desperate, I surrender
to belief
in glorious endings.

Forty

The interstate that

    runs east to west (or is it west to east)
    the one Matt and the gang traveled
    to hear Innocence Mission
    (said the lead singer reminded him of me),

    later took us to Montreat to hear Charlie Peacock
    where the dark-haired boy came up to me after, smiled,
    said *don't I know you from somewhere?*

    connects to I75 down to The Masquerade in Atlanta
    upstairs heaven, downstairs hell,
    standing room only while we crammed toward the stage
    to absorb the sound of Toad the Wet Sprocket
    not quite understanding lyrics like
    flesh becomes water, wood becomes bone
    but drawn in by the words all the same

             ***

The number of days

    (and nights) it rained,
    flooded the earth

    the spies searched Canaan,

    God gave Nineveh to repent

    Christ was tempted in the desert

    between resurrection and ascension

***

The years

   Moses lived before he killed an Israelite,

   he hid before returning
     to lead Israel out of Egypt

   they wandered in the desert
     eating bread from heaven

***

The age Ted would be, his birthday
   nipping at the heels of mine in a few short months
   if he had lived

Twice the years since I stood outside the college cafeteria
   with Becky and Brian, planned a trip
   to see Ted in the hospital
   a trip we would never have
   the chance to take

***

Weeks a baby gestates
   cocooned before entering the world

***

My mother's age when she first wore bifocals

***

Halfway to eighty, not as old as I once believed
   when my five-year-old self planned
   to be a grandmother

***

My age now,
   when we choose to foster
   waiting newborns
   give our time and hearts
   to little strangers
   like someone else did
   while we waited for our son

***

The age Jim said
   he would gladly wait until
   to start a family –
   words that broke my heart,
   and he was almost right, two years shy
   of his milestone birthday
   when our first miracle arrived
   and rendered that number
   relative

Beginning

in writing class the day after our adoption home study approval

Assigned to write
about someone from my past,
all I can think
is of my future.

In place of memories
I have questions.

Who will our baby be?
When will I meet him?
Will she look like me,
have my sense of humor?
Will he be a preemie
with fragile lungs?
Will she have ten
pink toes and fingers?
Will I hold him
his first day on earth?

What if the day never comes,
my present never catches up with
my future?

Moments tick by.
Time is not constant,
it flexes and stretches,
plays tricks on me.

Is that how it will be when I meet you?
Caught in a single moment,
and then, suddenly,
weeks and months will have passed?

Will you know how much
those moments matter,
the ones you can't remember?

Gestation

Instead of
my baby bump
we have a paper
clip art baby we call
Baby B angled against a
cabinet by the fireplace, a
reminder to act as parents-to-
be, who elicits questions, grins
from social workers, family, friends.

Instead of loose tops and stretchy pants,
I wear my own version of maternity clothes,
t-shirts that say *paper pregnant* and *Warning:*
I am in love with a child I haven't yet met.

Instead of an ultrasound, we create Happy
Baby Registration Day, complete with
balloons and streamers, replacements
for more typical milestones, tangible
reminders of who we trust will
make us a family of three.

My Son's Story

The shock of your arrival
made me giddy,
exuberant,
in the midst of sleep
deprivation,
your sudden entrance
a high
I had never known.

Your ten-day
old-man face,
your widow's peak,
wide brown eyes
lured me in.

Euphoria and belonging
mingled and blurred
those first hours, days
as I fed you,
changed you,
rocked you to sleep,
wondered
if your other mother
might come
to claim you.

But I let myself fall
  hard
    fast
in love precisely
as I imagined
and nothing
like it at all.

On the Verge of Sleep

He cries against my shoulder
as my drowsy head
nods and bobs

There is a wildness about him
in the night
arms flailing, lungs gusting

But then
he curls his tiny body
into the shape I imagine he bore

in his birth mother's womb
cocooned there
almost eight months' time

Asleep at last
I lay him down
climb into my bed

dissolve into dreams
where I hear him
cry out for me

Birthmother

Does she cry for him
at night
as he cries
for nourishment
and I cry
tears of joy?

Is there anyone
to share her grief?

Does she think
of milestones
I will witness,
ones for her
that won't exist –
first tooth
first scrape
first kiss

growing strong
independent...

As I sink back to sleep
I whisper
prayers of peace
for this stranger
who delivered
my wondrous gift.

Clear

My son stares out the window
dark eyes
entranced by the breeze-blown leaves
forgetting it's lunchtime.

Suddenly he's back again
mouth agape, a baby bird's
waiting for a spoonful of carrots,
his favorite.

He eats hungrily, eagerly.
I am not fast enough.
He reaches for the spoon
with both hands

grips it into his mouth
sucking, gumming,
drooling orange
through his toothless grin

and then the branches sway.
He lets go with mouth and fingers
to yet again be caught
by the Autumn wind.

Addition

once more
intent
to grow our family
we await another son,
perhaps a daughter

won't know when
or where
or who

fill out more forms
sit through interviews
classes
prove our worthiness
for second-time parenthood
bare ourselves
again

update our home study
meet with the social worker
wait for news

in time hear details
of a birth mother
who carries our precious
second child,
a mother
I will pray for in the dark

another woman we will
never have the chance
to thank

The Measure of Love

what is a heart for
if not to fill it full
to overflowing

to pour out multiplied
and love a second tiny stranger
uncertain, eager
for another set
of tiny toes

how long before I discover
detached earlobes
or a birth-marked shoulder

each day
a counting game
each trill of my phone
a question mark

is this the day
we become parents again,
our son
becomes a brother?

another mother
answers our prayer
for an additional child to love

and what is the cost
but this woman's
heart divided?

My Daughter's Story

The moment
I heard
your history

your story before
you were born
I fell

in love with you,
fell hard,
so hard

left the meeting with
our social worker
sat in the car

wept at what
you'd already
endured

shed silver tears
knowing soon
I'd be yours

Claiming

Thirty days
exactly
after our updated
home study is approved
we get a text
saying you are born
but won't know for
two days more
that you're a girl
our social worker
keeping your identity
a secret.

Because your brother has a cold
the day we meet you
I fear the agency
will make us wait
to bring you home
(a silly fear)
but then the social worker
places you
in my arms.
I lift you to my shoulder
and you spit up on me
brand me as your own.

You love to hear us tell
of hours later
when we walk the steps
to your grandparents' front door.
Grandma flings it wide, asks
Is it a boy or girl?

A grin on his sweet face
little J teases.
A boy, he says
as we lift a cover from the car seat,
reveal a pink-bowed headband
in your wavy black hair.

At home
we spread a blanket
on the floor
lay you down
beside your brother
who builds a train track
right around you –
when finished, he leans in
kisses the top of your head
the only way he knows
to claim you
as his own.

Secure

At two a.m. I hear your whimpers
hurry to feed you
before you wake
your big brother
in his room next to yours

Bleary-eyed, I almost trip
on a lump at my feet in the hall –
your brother huddled with his blanket
fast asleep, a silent sentry
If I move him, he will wake

so I step over him,
rock while you suck your bottle dry
put you back to bed
whisper a goodnight to you
and the guard on duty at your door

J's Prayer

I walk the hall to my room, weary,
spinning, swirling, sinking

>I hear my not yet three-year-old pray
>over his stuffed animals
>the way we pray
>for him at bedtime

I pause outside his room,
not quite depleted, but so exhausted

>*Tank you Big Brown Bear*
>*keep him safe, healfy*
>*tank you Iz's kitty cat*
>*she share with me*

I lean my head against his door,
listen to his soft voice

>*Tank you Padgetts, Hinkelmans*
>*Ama and Ampa*
>*please they come my house for supper*
>*have pancakes*

I breathe slow, breathe deep,
marvel at the simplicity of his requests

Devoted

after Eamon Grennan's *Opposing Forces*

I'm yours
they seem to say
these tiny faces
pressed against the window
noses smudging icy glass

they are not my flesh
but theirs
is a tender claim
holding on to me

a love so sharp
it takes my breath
away

40 mph

What's the speed limit?
my son asks me
as he and his sister chase
each other around the kitchen
table rolling mini backpacks
behind them.

Two miles per hour,
I say, hoping to slow them down.
He deserts his backpack
to stand beside me at the counter
as I chop onions, garlic, celery.

I think it's forty, he says,
impish grin on his face.
Can I have some onion?

Not to be left out
my baby girl toddles over
points to herself, mouth open.

You want some too? I ask.
Ya, she says with one huge nod.

After supper I request my
after meal kiss,
its accompanying thank-you,
a ritual since my son was old
enough to pucker.

My daughter willingly plants
messy, fragrant kisses on my cheek,
tries to catch and eat
the ones I blow her.

My son, however, has become
reluctant, choosing instead to deposit
his kisses in my pocket, *to save
for later*, he says.

Sixteen kisses, he told me
the other day.

Not near enough to last me
through his childhood.

Birth Day

Five years and one hour ago,
just after midnight,
unbeknownst to us
you drew your first breath
entered this world
but not my world.
I don't remember

the mundane happenings
of that Tuesday,
the days that followed,
unaware those days had
changed my life
until ten days later I first
saw your face
cradled your fragile body.

What must this anniversary be
for the woman who gave you
life, who carried you
around the world
in her womb before you
were placed in my arms
forever my son?

Today you build towers
and trains
play the guitar
plan to conquer the world
in another five years
as I watch and wonder
at the privilege I have
to claim you as my own.

Phonics Wars

Look, Daddy.
I drew the Million Falcon.

J looks at his father, eyes eager,
hands splayed on oversized paper
that covers half the table.

I see.
That looks great.

And here's R2D2.
J's finger rests on a robot
neat in its own square.

Next he points to the top corner,
another tidy label by a ship.

His daddy looks at his spelling,
and the corners
of his mouth turn up.

See, Daddy.
It's the Dust Star.

Discovery

can we go on a nature walk?
my almost three-year-old daughter asks
her vocabulary almost matching
her five-year-old brother's

we gather shoes, camera, buckets,
head out the door,
collect rocks, sticks, maple leaves,
a piece of bark
a yellow buttercup ripped
from the ground still sporting
roots

we kneel, touch, look, listen
point out birds and bugs, lizards and beetles

almost back at our door we spy
a caterpillar

my son, not the adventurer,
stoops low, studies the length
of dark fuzz
you can touch him, I say

his hand is gentle
an invitation

we sit in our driveway
ten minutes, fifteen perhaps,
as the caterpillar climbs, crawls, squirms
on little fingers

I've never seen my boy so absorbed
by a *living* thing
his face the same expression
as the day we brought him home
and the study of his world began

eventually, we go inside,
wash hands, eat lunch
forget about the wonder
of our bucket treasures

days later, outside riding bikes,
I see my daughter lift
her plastic trike
high above her head
slam it against concrete again
and again
a war cry on her lips

why are you squashing the bug, I ask

her trike mid-air, brown eyes wide,
she looks at me, her face a mask
of innocence
he not like it?

no, I say, *would you like it
if someone squashed you?*

my kids giggle, amused by the thought
of something large enough
to smash them like a bug,
ride off, their squeals and laughter
floating along behind them

Eat

I want a baby cat
my four-year-old tells me.
She asks for a kitten
almost every week.

I tell her how when I was little
I had a pet
who had to live outside, how
my big brother, her Uncle Randy,
day after day
found my cat, rubbed him in his face
until his eyes turned red and puffy.

Then went inside and told my mom,
Look what sister's cat did to me.

My daughter and her big brother think
it's a good joke
even though my kitty ran away.

We talk of other pets.
Guinea pigs. Fish. Turtles.
Their father suggests
we raise rabbits
for meat.
Keep two as pets.
Eat the rest.

I'm okay with the idea.
Except for the butchering.
And the kids are excited about the prospect
in their naïve way.

Again, my daughter asks for a kitten.
What if you *are allergic*? I ask.
She sits up straight, unfazed.
Then we can eat it.

Tethered

I heft my camera out of its bag,
my companion long before the arrival
of this long-awaited daughter,
hang the strap around my neck.

My five-year-old girl pleads
to come outside,
take pictures of her own,
her newfound joy the capture of an image.

I smile, hand her the iPad,
and we walk into the setting sun,
turn our focus to tiny blue flowers
I can't identify that sprout in the mulch,

zinnias, cosmos, swallowtails,
the slant of light across a fallen oak leaf,
the shadow of a Deodar Cedar by the playset
as my shadow follows me.

Paul

my mother's father

I hear your sandpaper voice
worn smooth
from a century of use

as I watch my son,
your single syllable
his middle name.

He sees you as his yardstick
to measure
what has happened in his world.

Was Great Grandpa alive then?
he asks, as we talk of ancient Greece,
butter churns, winter sleighs.

His voice grows strong and true
as sand slips through your hourglass,
wears your voice

away.

Elizabeth

my father's mother

Separated from me by
a generation
a culture,
distance,

my grandmother
never scrubbed her pots and pans
until they shone

but cleaned them
with efficiency,
moved on to the next thing to be done

Her Kitchenaid, Imperial Gray,
(the color I insisted on when I bought mine)
mixed chocolate,
fudge,

batter
for sheet
after sheet
of cookies for market

I hear her hum this morning
in my memory
this stranger
who was flesh and blood,

her voice etched
by decade
after decade of use

What would she think
of my dark-eyed daughter,
not born of me,
who hums her way through each day

like the great-grandmother
she will never know

Memory

I won't remember
the last time
my son holds my hand in public,
slips his hand in
and out, unsure
if he still wants his fingers
nestled against mine.

I remember
the day we met him,
the hour before when we were told
he was alive, in this world,
soon to be in mine, how I knew
he would be beautiful
as soon as the social worker told us
he was Filipino.

I don't remember
what happened
the day he was born,
only the few notes in my journal,
a dream I had that night
about a call from the agency
that our baby was born.

I do remember
a dream years earlier
about adopting
a Laotian boy,
a dream so real I woke,
told my husband we needed
to get on a plane to Laos
that very day.

Invitation

Momma, when can we schedule your ballet lesson?
It's part of your birthday present, you know

> My daughter, impatient, asks me to check my calendar
> so she can tutor me in plies, jetés, tendues,
> things she has learned from a DVD,
> now claims as her expertise

I stand behind the couch, our makeshift barre,
follow her example

> She encourages me to try a split –
> a skill she has almost perfected
> in her youthful flexibility

I grip the couch, slide one foot until
I'm holding on for dear life,
my body nowhere near the floor

> *You're doing so much better, Momma*
> *You're this much closer*

She holds her hands several inches apart,
far more than the millimeters I may have gained
in the weeks since her instruction began

> (How long will she continue to invite me
> to her living room dance academy,
> ask me to join her in her world?)

With my arms I haul myself to standing
wrap them around my girl,

and though I know I'll fail,
determine to accept
as many invitations
as she offers

Resemblance

I glance across the table
at my niece's cherub face,
her hair of fire-born gold
the color mine used to be

this brother's daughter
who doesn't belong to me

I used to dream I had
an auburn-haired girl,
eyes the color of sky
to match her daddy's

and yet, when I look at my daughter
I don't often note our differences

I see her sense of humor
so much like her daddy's
I imagine it must be genetic,

a tender spirit so much
like mine was
as a child –

how could she not come from me?

How could any other child fit
this daughter space
within me that holds her shape
and hers alone?

Invisible Wounds

I grieve the distance
our wounds (the ones we brought
into marriage, the ones acquired since)
have put between us
our fingers sometimes brushing

then a gaping fissure forms,
so I can hardly see you.

***

You should adopt a baby due in September
the social worker says when I take our foster baby
to the agency to meet his family.
We're too old, I tell her.
You're young enough, she says.
He's due in two months' time.
Start your paperwork, send it in.

I still grieve the children I never
had the chance to bear

this child due soon you say I cannot have
the one I didn't know I wanted,
this desire for another child
a separate yearning from my previous one
to carry a child within my womb.

***

We sit together as a family
turn to the next Bible story which speaks
of Abraham and Sarah. Though advanced in age
they bore a son, called him Isaac
which means laughter
the name I have given to this baby boy
we decided we can't adopt, the baby I will never meet
who perhaps took his first breath last week,

severed from his mother's world to be placed forever
in another woman's arms, heart.

Not mine.

But that's not
quite true.
Because he has lived in my heart, mind,
since mid-July when words of his existence
were first spoken to me, words that sliced
open an old wound I believed to be long healed,
cutting through scar tissue more tender than I imagined,
down to my core.

***

We are broken,
both in need of mending
so how do I lay down this burden
sewn into the center of my being,
so embedded it will always be a part of me,
how do I walk the tight-rope across our chasm
meet you where you are
when my eyes are full of tears?

***

I wonder if he's arrived,
if his birth mother is okay, who his new family is,
if he's brought laughter.
I think of my children's birth mothers,
faces from photographs
two days after they gave birth,
two women who carried treasure in their wombs,
then said goodbye.

***

And now my baby girl, at six, asks
why do some birth mothers
give their babies away?
Why did mine?
And I don't have adequate answers,
never will, because, like us, humanity is fallen
fraught with shame and secrets and hard choices
cervical ribs and endometriosis and infertility
grief and loss and loneliness and isolation
and pain and envy and forgiveness
and trust and salvation and my cup running over
compassion and passion and an ache that
goes on forever
none of which show visible scars, but cut deep
honing, refining, purifying
painful in ways I can't explain.

***

But then there's the blue of your eyes,
the way your lashes frame them,
even if hidden behind glasses.
I used to gaze into those eyes, take stock of how we were.
Those eyes used to gaze back, really see me.

How did I lose sight of blue?

I blame it on the busy-ness of life,
longed-for children begging time and attention,
gadgets that interfere with what used to pass for conversation.

Even if they don't hold my gaze
as long as they once did,
I've started, once again, to pay attention.
To see your eyes.
See you.

Found

I didn't sense the loss
of our foster baby
the moment I placed him
in his new mother's arms,
knew only the joy I saw
on her face,
his tiny body held
in her embrace.

It wasn't until
the next day,
the gray day after,
as I watched my children
grieve his absence,
that I began to feel
the lack of him.

And yet, it wasn't just
the letting go of *him*,
but the final, solid
closing of a door
long left open,
if only an inch,

the realization
we are truly finished
with the forming
of *our* family.
No more
first grins,
first teeth,
first steps.

It hit me
with a force
for which I was wholly
unprepared,
this new grief so similar
to the old one, as if
best friends
comparing notes.

Once again I learn
to surrender,
not lose myself
in grief, but let my grief
be lost.

About the Author

Cheryl Boyer is a writer and novice shutterbug whose work has appeared in a handful of journals, including *Kakalak*, *The Main Street Rag*, and *moonShine review*. She lives in a small town in North Carolina with her husband and two children, is a home-schooling momma, and a sometime foster mom.

Cheryl truly discovered the beauty of poetry when she began writing in the midst of infertility, but her joy of the written word was instilled when her third grade teacher chose her to be part of a creative writing class.

Though not a coffee drinker, Cheryl finds it essential to eat a bit of dark chocolate every day.

Website: www.myferriswheel.com
Email:cheryl@myferriswheel.com